LOONY LIMERICKS

from Alabama to Wyoming

LOONY LIMERICKS

from ALABAMA
to WYOMING

written and illustrated by

JACK STOKES

DOUBLEDAY & COMPANY, INC., GARDEN CITY, NEW YORK

ISBN 0-385-12916-5 Trade
0-385-12917-3 Prebound
Library of Congress Catalog Card Number 77–10304

Dedicated to Jeff, Eve, and Abby.
You have every right to feel crabby.
	It could not be debated,
	While this book was created,
The treatment you've had has been shabby.

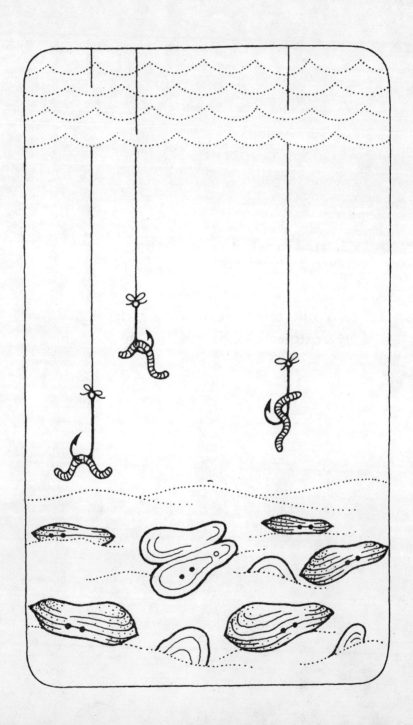

Alabama

A fat woman from Alabama
Had her heart set on being in drama.
    Although at her size
    It was no surprise
When she ended in wide Cinerama.

An entrepreneur from Mobile
Thought oysters would earn a great deal.
    But the profits were slim
    Since no one told him
They're not caught with a rod and a reel!

Alaska

A man moved from France to Alaska.
He had lived in Peru and Nebraska.
    Before that Cape Horn—
    As to where he was born,
He says, "I am glada you aska!"

There's an arrogant scholar from Juneau
Who is sure that he knows more than you know.
    His very best friend
    Is the absolute end.
He knows he knows more than you two know.

Arizona

    A husband from Page, Arizona,
    Had a wife by the name of Winonah.
        His first name is Jonah,
        He took out Ramona,
    Now he has to hide out in Daytona!

    A bandit was captured in Tucson
    When he thought the police had a truce on.
        He was sent to the chair
        But he didn't care
    As long as no one turned the juice on!

Arkansas

A Marcus Nijinsky from Arkansas
Went out for a walk in the dark n'saw
    Lots of goblins and ghouls
    And a green thing that drools.
He fainted and that is all Marc N. saw!

California

Out in beautiful old California
There's one fault and I'm trying to warn ya.
    If the earth starts to shake
    And they have a big quake,
Only heirs that are left come to mourn ya!

A girl went to try Hollywood.
She had talent that was jolly good.
    She could dance, act, and sing.
    Though her phone did not ring,
She did more than a tired collie could.

Colorado

A cowpoke in Cortez, Colorado,
Tried to look like a fierce desperado.
    But he didn't scare us
    With all of his fuss—
No one ever was killed by bravado!

An exquisite maid from Pike's Peak
Got herself in a horrible pique.
    When she went to change clothes
    And powder her nose
Her neighbor was trying to peek!

Connecticut

A charming young thing in Connecticut
Was taught all the rules of good etiquette.
    I thought she would die
    When she saw that I
Used my fingers to hold the croquette I cut.

There was a new student at Yale,
Who spent all his time drinking ale.
    Never opened a book
    For exams that he took.
After seeing his grades he looked pale!

Delaware

A dapper young man who's from Delaware
Has impeccable taste he is well aware.
 He's been asked to come dine
 With some nudists at nine,
So he's pondering, "What should a fella wear?"

Florida

 A magnificent Florida man
 Decided to get a good tan.
  He went out on a raft
  Till a shark came up aft.
 Now he sells by the ounce in a can!

A chick who was born in Key West
Thought the living there really was best,
 But the last hurricane
 Swept away her domain
And Quebec is her present address.

In Florida's vast Everglades
Live several pretty young maids.
    They are the curators
    For mean alligators,
So not even one of them wades.

Georgia

A mouse from Atlanta, GA,
Was fond of a cat that was gray.
  He asked it to play
  And to his dismay
Found fondness in more than one way!

In a swamp called the Okefenokee
There's a monster inclined to be pokey.
  He lies in the sun
  And ignores everyone,
But by me that is just okey dokey!

Hawaii

Hawaii's a hard word to rhyme,
So if I go on wasting my time
  Attempting to write
  A verse that is bright,
I probably won't make a dime.

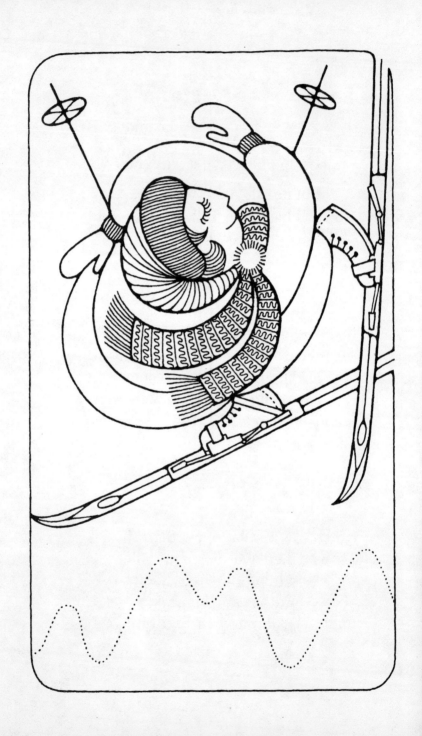

A mongoose from near Diamond Head
Is sad that the snakes are all dead.
    He did a good job
    But he said, with a sob,
"Now I'll have to eat lizards instead!"

Idaho

A vigorous Idaho girl
Thought she would give skiing a whirl.
    When she took her first jump,
    She came down with a thump.
Now they're waiting for her to uncurl!

A swinger who's from Pocatello
Tried a diet of whiskey and jello.
    Though his silhouette shows it
    I don't think he knows it,
But he goes around feeling quite mellow!

Illinois

An exceedingly nearsighted boy
Went hunting in north Illinois.
    It was his kind of luck
    When he shot at a duck,
That he wounded his nicest decoy!

A woman who came from Decatur
Set out to explore the equator,
    Found a snake she adored
    But its meals she ignored,
So while she was sleeping it ate'er!

Indiana

There's a goat from Fort Wayne, Indiana,
Eats his cans with a titch of banana.
    As a finishing touch
    He adds an old clutch
And a smidgen of shredded bandanna!

A friend who has lived in South Bend
Will defend this advice he has penned.
   "If there's money to spend,
    But no money to lend,
There's a poor dividend in the end!"

Iowa

In Iowa there was a tractor
That wanted to be a great actor,
   But he blew the audition
    When he stripped his ignition,
And that was a terminal factor.

Two partners that came from Des Moines
Tried making a counterfeit coin.
   In Washington's place
    One put his own face
And now they have cells that adjoin!

Kansas

There's a shrink who is living in Kansas
And we wonder if he understands us.
    When our problems get deep
    He drops off to sleep,
But look at the bill that he hands us!

In the earliest days of Dodge City
If your draw was not fast 'twas a pity.
On the stone at your head
The inscription that said
Something sad was so apt to be witty!

Kentucky

A colonel who lived in Kentucky
Was inspired with a thought that was lucky.
He loved cooking chicken
And liked finger lickin',
So now he is selling fried clucky!

If you're touring way down Mammoth Cave
Then you really should not misbehave.
You could wander astray
Or you might lose your way
And the prospect is certainly grave!

Louisiana

In Louisiana, a kid
Who liked to eat crayfish and squid
    Consumed all he could,
    Much more than he should.
All night he regretted he did!

A raven that came from Monroe
Could talk and appeared on a show.
    His answers were wrong.
    He didn't last long.
You might say he had to eat crow!

Maine

When a little old lady from Maine
Tried to build a low-cost hydroplane,
    She had no way to steer
    And forgot reverse gear.
That's why she is living in Spain.

A nasty old bear up in Bangor
Was suffering feelings of anger.
    They called in advisors
    And tried tranquilizers.
Now he lies around basking in languor.

Maryland

A skydiver jumped over Maryland,
Thought the view looked a lot like a fairyland.
    But the cord did not work
    When he gave it a jerk,
And now he is part of that very land!

    Some Washington folks from D.C.
    Try to give away everything free.
        When they run out of money,
        It might not be funny.
    I'm afraid they will give away me!

Massachusetts

A dowager living in Mass.
Was just simply reeking with class,
    But it was so obscene
    When her finger turned green
From a ring that was made out of brass!

There's a man who loved fish from Cape Cod;
He ate almost nothing but scrod.
>When he grew shiny scales
>And played with the whales,
Only tourists considered him odd!

A maid living near Plymouth Rock
Made herself a complete laughingstock.
>As she posed by a loom
>In a Pilgrim's costume,
She was wearing hot pants, not a frock!

Michigan

The wife of a sportsman in Michigan
Said she would not clean any fish again.
>But if in the spring
>He brings home a string,
I bet she will cook one more dish again.

There's a talented man from Detroit,
At designing he's very adroit.
　　He devised a new car
　　Shaped like a guitar,
But it really is hard to exploit!

Minnesota

There was a shy boy out in Minn.
And he had an identical twin.
　　While they looked just the same,
　　If they courted a dame,
He looked sad while his brother would grin!

There's a devious man from Duluth
Who simply cannot tell the truth.
　　He's no friend of King Kong
　　Nor the champ of Ping-pong
And we know that his name is not Ruth!

Mississippi

A boy from Yazoo, Mississippi,
Didn't know that the boats were so tippy.
    His date tried to stand,
    They turned over and
Now each thinks the other is drippy!

There was a wee prankster in Natchez
Who wouldn't stop playing with matches.
    He set fire to his clothes
    And now everyone knows
The hair on his head all detaches!

Missouri

A pretty young miss from Missouri
Decided to cook with some curry.
    Without knowledge of such,
    She guessed at how much,
Now her eyeballs are red and all furry!

Though they seem very friendly and homey,
In Joplin they shrug and say, "Show me."
　　This lack of some trust
　　Doesn't seem to be just.
You wouldn't suppose that they know me?

Montana

There's a matronly woman named Anna
Who has never been out of Montana.
    Though she likes the locale
    She is never banal
'Cause she puffs on cigars from Havana!

A competent man lives in Billings.
He's an expert and famous for drillings.
    He turned down a job
    From a dentist named Bob
As he's drilling for oil and not fillings!

Nebraska

In Nebraska a handsome young farmer
Was known everywhere as a charmer.
    An experienced lady
    Thought perhaps he was shady,
So she had a new dress made of armor!

Nevada

An ex-sailor who lives in Nevada
Thought he'd like to command an armada.
    Lacking ships or a sea
    Is the reason why he
Sails oat flakes in a cup of Salada.

Although Reno is known for divorce,
There are gambling casinos of course.
    You can lose all your dough
    Which will then only show
There is more than one path to remorse!

New Hampshire

A native way up in New Hampshire
When asked 'bout his state said, "I am sure
    Our scenery is splendid,
    But when fall is ended,
It gets very cold, that's for damn sure!"

Long the shoreline of Winnipesaukee
The sport in the winter is hockey,
    But it's not very nice
    If you fall through the ice.
It is cold, very wet, and quite rocky!

New Jersey

A man in Secaucus, N.J.
Fed thousands of pigs every day.
   When the sun got too hot,
   Believe it or not,
Even he was seen running away!

A smarty from Asbury Park
Went out for a walk in the dark.
   He was naked of clothes
   From his toes to his nose,
But his derby eliminates stark!

New Mexico

The handsomest catch in New Mexico
Filled the tank of his Jaguar with Texaco
   And put the top down
   As he roared out of town.
The ladies were sad to see sexy go!

A man from around Albuquerque
Whose mind had become a bit murky
    Really hated November
    And the end of December
Because he thought he was a turkey!

New York

There's a glutton that lived in New York
Whose favorite meat was roast pork.
    While his bites were gigantic
    His howling grew frantic
When he found he had swallowed the fork!

A fool at Niagara Falls
Tried to make it across using crawls.
    He went over the edge
    And was found with a dredge,
But it took more than ninety-one hauls!

North Carolina

A girl who's from North Carolina
Bought a bird that can talk; it's a myna!
   Though at first we were cheering,
   Now we're all tired of hearing
It sing, "Is there anyone finah?"

There once was a pitiful collie
That lived on the outskirts of Raleigh.
   No one called him a felon
   When he sneaked watermelon.
They all knew he's a bit melancholy.

North Dakota

Some residents in North Dakota
Really don't even care an iota
   When it starts to snow,
   Although we all know
They often get more than their quota.

Ohio

There's a co-ed that lived in Ohio.
When she saw her beau she would sigh, "Oh."
    If you don't know why,
    It can only imply
That you never studied your bio.

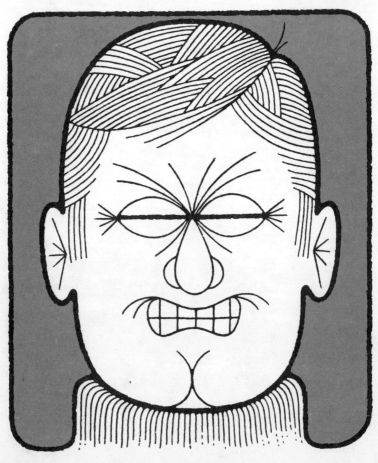

An old woman from Cincinnati
Who was just a little bit batty
    Ate a used hockey puck
    And then died—rotten luck.
She thought t'was a hamburger patty!

Oklahoma

There are places throughout Oklahoma
Where the cattle cause quite an aroma.
    Don't inhale it too deep,
    It will put you to sleep.
One fellow went into a coma.

An impractical man they call Vinton
Tried to watch an eclipse over Clinton.
    He looked at the sun
    From noon until one,
And the rest of the day he was squintin'!

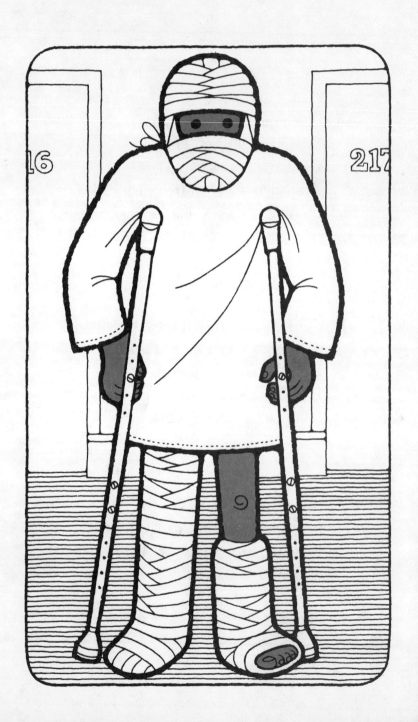

Oregon

There's a fisherman living in Oregon;
One morning he found his new dory gone.
    His wife named Lorraine
    Rowed off with a swain.
He is sad with his dory and Lorrie gone.

    A man living near Crater Lake,
Having trouble with keeping awake,
    Didn't stay in his bed
    But went swimming instead,
And that was a fatal mistake!

Pennsylvania

A worker from Pittsburgh, PA,
Tried making his own Chevrolet.
    He had all the parts,
    But he didn't have smarts.
He'll be off of his crutches in May!

A historian living in Reading
Thought he'd like to attend a beheading.
    When he was the one
    To whom it was done,
It was the last thing he was dreading.

Rhode Island

A hobo that came from Rhode Island
Went to Scotland to visit the Highland.
    He agreed it was nice,
    But he likes rice,
So now he is living in Thailand.

South Carolina

A rather poor student named Dinah
Lived somewhere in South Carolina.
    She flunked her geography
    And cinematography
When she thought Rin Tin Tin was in China!

CHANGCHUN ●

PEKING ●

LANCHOW
●

CHINA

RIN TIN TIN ★

SHANGHAI ●

●
CHUNGKING

FOOCHOW ●

CANTON
●

A beautiful belle down in Sumter
Was puzzled when her lover dumped her.
    She had changed her mouthwash
    And her soap too, by gosh!
His leaving has certainly stumped her.

South Dakota

A fig lover from South Dakota
Insisted that they be Kadota.
    No one ever knew why
    He had all he could buy
In the trunk of his purple Toyota!

There's a ghost flies around Aberdeen.
He goes under, above, and between.
    Though his hair's in distress
    And his nails are a mess,
No one knows as he never is seen!

Tennessee

A farmer who lived down in Tenn.
Was known for his polka-dot hen.
    She laid eggs that were striped
    And when customers griped,
She just cackled and did it again!

A collector who's from Chattanooga
Has a car that he bought in Tortuga.
    It is awfully old,
    Though you needn't be told
When he honks and it goes ooga ooga!

Texas

A little old maid down in Texas
Was very confused about sexes;
    Thought a bull was somehow
    Just the same as a cow.
Her error will always perplex us!

A cowboy is living in Dallas.
His name may seem strange but it's Alice.
    Betsy-Ann is his brother.
    Put the blame on their mother,
Though neither bear her any malice.

Utah

A marble contestant from Utah
Who watched himself losing in mute awe
    Thought the game wasn't fun—
    His competitor won—
And all he has left is his new taw.

A visitor swam in Salt Lake.
He made a regretful mistake
    By drinking the water
    When he hadn't oughter
And getting a bad bellyache!

Vermont

There's a very sly swain in Vermont
Who has all the girls he could want.
    If one gets too serious,
    He looks so mysterious
And says, "I am married and cahn't!"

Virginia

A beautiful belle from VA
Found a hair that had started to gray,
  So she used a new tint
  Without reading the print—
You must see her lovely toupee!

A gourmet from Chesapeake Bay
Ate oysters almost every day,
  But he had to eat clams
  With cole slaw and yams
During August, July, June, and May.

Washington

'Bout the westernmost section of Washington
You will hear lots of humorous joshing done.
  But the rains are not funny
  'Cause when it's not sunny,
Many people can't get any washing done.

58

A girl who lived near Puget Sound
Liked the water much more than the ground.
 She went for a stroll
 On the water, poor soul,
If successful, she wouldn't have drowned!

West Virginia

A teacher who's from West Virginia
Says, "I'll get some intelligence in ya.
　　If you don't get the pitch,"
　　He says twirling his switch,
"Then I'm warning you now, I will skin ya!"

There was a big woman in Wheeling
Whose head almost came to the ceiling.
　　As I seem to recall
　　I am nearly as tall
But only because she is kneeling!

A patron at White Sulphur Springs
Did the most inconsiderate things.
　　She brought on some wrath
　　When leaving the bath
Because it was covered with rings!

Wisconsin

A little old maid from Wisconsin
Who finally married a Johnson
    Decided his smoking
    Was causing her choking.
She's carefully hidden his Ronson!

There's a limerick concerning Racine
Saying things that are not very clean.
    I think it's a pity
    As it's a nice city
And the person who wrote it is mean!

Wyoming

A bachelor girl from Wyoming,
Whose hair always needed some combing,
    She had dates after dinner
    'Cause she could have been thinner,
But she looked pretty good in the gloaming!

There's a very sad goose out in Lander
Who's becoming an object of slander.
    She doesn't lay eggs,
    Though everyone begs.
No one knows that the goose is a gander!

JACK STOKES is a lively and fun-loving man who was born and raised in Ohio and now lives with his wife and three children in Old Lyme, Connecticut. A free-lance designer and illustrator since 1966, he has done illustrations for advertising as well as for Xerox's children's publications. He is the author and illustrator of LET'S CATCH A FISH and MIND YOUR A's AND Q's and has several other books in varying stages of progress. When not writing or illustrating books, Mr. Stokes keeps busy preserving old architecture, doing amateur landscaping, taking long walks on the beach, and telling terrible jokes to anyone who will listen.